DARK PSYCHOLOGY SECRETS

How to Influence People To Positive Behavior In
Relationship With NLP

BENEDICT GOLEMAN

not engaging in the rendering of legal, financial, medical or professional advice. The content within this book has been derived from various sources. Please consult a licensed professional before attempting any techniques outlined in this book.

By reading this document, the reader agrees that under no circumstances is the author responsible for any losses, direct or indirect, which are incurred as a result of the use of information contained within this document, including, but not limited to, errors, omissions, or inaccuracies.

Table of Contents

INTRODUCTION 8

CHAPTER 1: THE PRESENCE OF PSYCHOLOGY IN OUR BEHAVIORS 11

CHAPTER 2: WHEN PSYCHOLOGY TURNS DARK 20

CHAPTER 3: WHAT IS NLP? 27

    Neuro-Linguistic Programming 28

    The Keys to NLP 32

    The History of NLP 39

CHAPTER 4: NLP BASIC PRINCIPLES TO IMPROVE LIFE 44

    Know your outcome 45

    Take action 49

    Sensory acuity 50

    Behavioral Flexibility 53

    Physiology of excellence 55

CHAPTER 5: NLP MIND CONTROL 58

    What is Neuro-Linguistic Processing? 59

    NLP to Control Minds 61

    NLP and Mirroring 64

    NLP to Create Anchors 68

    NLP and Pace and Lead 71

CHAPTER 6: HYPNOSIS 74

    How Hypnosis Works 75

    Why Use Hypnosis? 78

        Using Hypnosis 80

        Bombardment 80

        Nonverbal Hypnosis 81

CHAPTER 7: THE BENEFITS OF DARK PSYCHOLOGY............................. 85

    Is Dark Psychology Evil?... 85

    Reasons to Use Dark Psychology 87

    The Insight of Dark Psychology.. 89

CHAPTER 8: NLP FOR A SUCCESSFUL LIFE 94

    Dissociation 96

    Content Reframing 98

    Anchoring Yourself 100

CONCLUSION 104

INTRODUCTION

Congratulations on purchasing **Dark Psychology Secrets** and thank you for doing so.

Have you ever wondered why some of the most insidious people on the planet are somehow able to charm everyone to fall for their every whim? Think of serial killers like Ted Bundy—he was commonly believed to be a handsome, charismatic young man that was able to quickly and easily win the favor of others almost naturally, and yet behind the scenes, he was a serial rapist and murderer of at least 30 homicides over a 4 year period of time. How did he do it? How was he able to sneak past so many people undetected for so long?

The answer is through dark psychology.

Many of the darkest personality types out there are quite capable of seeming charming and affable, only to be hiding the monster underneath their masks. This is a method they use to prey on other people, victimizing those who dare to fall for their charm. Dark psychology delves into these personality types, studying the underlying motivations for the behaviors at hand. This is not only to understand what to look out for when you are in the real world—when you learn to understand the minds of those with dark personalities, you can begin to claim their own ways of thinking.

CHAPTER 1: THE PRESENCE OF PSYCHOLOGY IN OUR BEHAVIORS

We love to think of ourselves as free thinkers—as people with complete and utter control over ourselves and what we do. We like to think that we have complete free will, and while we always have a choice to do something a certain way or another, one thing is certain: The choice to act in specific manners is primarily created through certain common thought patterns that control us and are not nearly as unique as you may think. Psychology is present in just about every aspect of what we do. It is there when we choose to integrate with other people. It is there as a guiding principle to everything that we do without exception. When you consider the fact that people tend to behave in patterns, no matter who they are, you realize that you can run into all sorts of problems. It is easy to think that you are unique—that you are not predictable. It is easy to think that you are someone that is not going to fall for the same patterns over and over, but the truth is, the presence of psychology is incredibly strong. Your actions that you take are easily explained—by psychology.

That's right—psychology is there at every turn, explaining everything. You can not only understand your own behaviors, but you can also begin to predict them or the behaviors of other people as well. This is because of the fact that you are a product of nature and biology, just like everyone else. You are the product of nature, and nature is something that can be explained if you know what you are looking at and understand how to begin to decode it. After all, we know that dogs put their tails down and growl when they are feeling threatened or if they are going to behave aggressively. We know this by understanding dogs in general. However, you can apply that information in other ways as well. You can apply that information to begin to see that other dogs when they put their tails down and growl, are also feeling threatened. Human psychology allows us to create the same sorts of inferences about human behavior so we can begin to recognize what it is that people do and why it happens in those patterns.

With psychology, you can explain how people learn—how people choose to behave. Imagine this situation: A child is bitten by a dog, and the child grows up to be terrified by dogs. This is explained by psychology. You can look at how emotions are created, and in this case, fear is created due to the thoughts of dogs being threats. Fear is created by those negative associations. By understanding how fear is created, we can also start understanding how fear can be overcome as well. This means that with our understanding of people and the working of the human mind, we can recognize everything that we do.

Every single behavior that you have can be explained by psychology in one way or another, whether it is explaining how you act or how you chose to react. These are different— actions are behavioral choices that you create while reactions are those that are responses to what you are doing. When you start to recognize the importance of psychology and why it matters so much to follow along with understanding it, you realize that learning to understand the reasons that you behave the way that you do is integral to living life to its fullest. If you know that you are likely to get defensive reactions when you, for example, tell someone something in certain ways, you can learn to work around it.

Learning to see that really, the behaviors that we naturally gravitate toward are little more than predictable tendencies becomes imperative. It provides you with the understanding that nothing that you do is without reason—there is a purpose behind every single action that see someone else do. It also opens the door for all sorts of other understanding as well. It is the case that you can use psychology to not only understand yourself and work with yourself, a skill known as emotional intelligence but also to understand others. You can learn to read your own tendencies to alter them into behaviors that are going to be more productive than they otherwise would be. You will see that you can begin to understand how to alter your way of thinking so you can be in control of any situation at hand.

Understanding psychology becomes a key concept for just about any aspect of human behavior. Whether being able to manipulate other people, read people's body language, or control yourself, you need to have a background in psychology to make it work. Now, that doesn't mean that you need to go out and spend an exorbitant amount of money to get a degree on the subject—but what you can do is read. You can do your due diligence just by learning through books and reading all about the information that exists. You can also learn by actively utilizing the information yourself as well— discovering through trial and efror what appens and howit works.

This book is just the beginning of a series on psychology. This book is the foundation of knowledge that you will need to know when it comes time to address everything else that you will see on the topics provided. As you read through the entire series, you will get all sorts of crucial information. We will begin by discussing human psychology and some crucial tenets that you must understand when looking further into the books in this series.

Dark psychology, the ability to draw from the psychology of dark individuals and apply it to others, regardless of the intention that you may have, is a skill that will teach you how to firmly plant people in the palm of your hand. Understanding the field of dark psychology allows you to not only avoid falling for the tactics that are used against you but also to begin to utilize those skills as well to influence people your own way. This is being capable of taking control and taking charge of powers that people such as sociopaths and narcissists regularly utilize to influence and control other people. It will allow you to use these tenets to begin to control what other people think—without them ever realizing that they are doing so. It is incredibly powerful and a skill that will take you far in life.

Psychology also becomes a key to understanding how to manipulate other people without them seeing it. You will be able to adjust the thinking of those around you just by virtue of understanding what you must do to navigate the world. We may know what we are going to do, and we may have complete control over ourselves, but we cannot maintain that control over other people as well. That control over others is much more fickle—for example, we can influence others, but there is no way for us to maintain complete control over them if we try to. It is impossible for us to be able to control someone the way we can control, for example, a video game character perfectly. However, we can still highly influence the behaviors that other people do. We can make it a point to change up how other people behave so we can begin to take control. There are so many ways that you can do so, and they are highly powerful. If you want to be able to do so, you can.

It also plays a significant role in explaining body language and how to analyze it in other people as well. Being able to read body language means that you are capable of understanding the true intentions of those around you, as well as granting you the power of being able to control people as well. Body language and being able to analyze others actually become key in being capable of controlling others. It allows you to influence other people without having to really think about it and without them realizing what you are doing either.

The understanding of psychology can also provide you with crucial information to begin to work on yourself as well. Through focusing on yourself and what you do over time, you can begin to understand precisely how you can work with yourself. You can see how you can start to improve upon your weaknesses or to recover from abuse, or you can see how you are likely to fall into similar traps of actions over and over again if you aren't careful. Being able to understand this information is crucial if you want to better yourself. Do you want to become more emotionally intelligent so you can thrive at work? You can do that through understanding the psychology that goes into it all. This information and this understanding will become your lifeline—it will become the way in which you can do everything. It will help you to improve yourself better. It will help you to become far more capable of successfully navigating your relationships.

Everything that you can learn about psychology becomes relevant to your day-to-day life if you know what to look for and how to connect the dots. It will help you to better control yourself and influence how you behave. It will help you to take control of others and understand and navigate the actions that you have far better than you thought possible. And it all begins with applying psychology to your behaviors so you can better interpret them. Remember, your thoughts, feelings, and behaviors are all linked together and, left to their own devices, will influence your entire life. You will be controlled by them if you do not take control of yourself.

Learning to recognize and accept this fact becomes a key tenet to your own success in navigating your own relationships in the future.

Psychology becomes one of the most important fields for you to study for this reason alone—when you learn to apply it, it can help you in just about every single situation that you will find yourself in. That is powerful—and it is imperative for you to learn. Learning to understand people so well will help you to make sure that you are perfectly capable of getting through just about any situation that you may find yourself within. You should be able to convince people to do exactly what you want if you know how to tap into their skills. Now, not everyone will be comfortable with this—not everyone will feel like controlling other people without feeling like they've done something wrong. Not everyone has the ruthlessness necessary to take control of other people and the important part is learning to recognize your own limits and what you are willing and unwilling to do.

CHAPTER 2: WHEN PSYCHOLOGY TURNS DARK

Dark psychology is a subset of psychology that you can utilize that draws from the understanding of how people who belong to the dark triad think. This is a triad of traits that are commonly applied to certain ways of thinking. They are people who rarely actually care about how people behave—they have little to no interest in being able to show others how they behave. They do not care about how people will be impacted by their behaviors—they just want to take control to get what benefits them above all else.

The dark triad refers to people with three key personality traits—narcissistic, Machiavellian, and sociopathic. Each of these alters the way that the individual will behave with other people. Those who are narcissistic typically lack the ability to influence how they interact with others. They may, for example, care more about themselves and getting what they want than making sure that they are fair to the other person. Typically, narcissists have very little care about other people—to them, they are the most important people in the world, and they will do whatever it takes to look out for Number One in their life.

Machiavellian people are those who believe that the ends will always justify the means. To them, people are disposable— they do not see a reason not to use other people if they can get away with it. They do not care just due to the fact that it doesn't matter to them. How other people feel is irrelevant just due to the fact that feelings are not going to help them. Machiavellian people swear by making sure that at the end of the day, they are taken care of. Everyone else becomes irrelevant in this case. They will usually utilize manipulation of other people with no qualms about what it would do to other people because, to them, it is irrelevant. After all, so long as they get to their destination, what happens to everyone else is unimportant.

Sociopaths are people that we commonly recognize as not having much of a moral compass, but there is more to it than that. Sociopaths know that something is wrong, and they may feel an inkling of guilt over it, but they do not care enough to stop what they are doing. They lack empathy, an incredibly dangerous trait to be lacking when it comes to interacting with people, and because of that, they are often found to be quite destructive. People, in lacking empathy, tend to use other people like tools because they see no reason not to. They see no reason that they would not be capable of influencing or controlling other people. As long as they make it happen, that's good enough for them.

When you take a look at dark psychology, you will be drawing from the psychology of these three people. They are all three known as master manipulators—they are incredibly skilled at being able to control others. They are incredibly powerful and able to do whatever it is that they need without qualms just due to the fact that they lack that empathy. Empathy is usually that ability that keeps us from hurting other people—it helps us to understand that other people have feelings too ad that we ought to respect them. It is that ability that we have to understand that we can tell how our actions will impact others and that we can use that power to help. However, when people lack that empathy, such as those who would fall into the Dark Triad, they lose that moral compass that would help them. They lose that ability that allows for proper socialization and proper interaction.

The manipulation that they use is highly potent and usually undetected by the victims. It is something that many want to tap into—it allows for an understanding of what can be done to control others. After all, manipulation is not negative in all forms—some forms can often be justified depending on the context solely due to the fact that nothing in the world is black and white.

Some people want to understand the skills that go into manipulating other people as thoroughly as the dark triad are able to do so. There are skills that go into it. There are ways that you can start to see how to influence others. You can see how other people act. You can see the strings that you can pull to control others, and you can use it to influence them. Others want to understand this topic because they want to be able to prevent themselves from being harmed instead. Either way, however, you start to see that being in control is highly important. Understanding how others work is something that can help you, no matter what it is that you are going to do with the knowledge. Remember, knowledge is power, and if you have that, you have everything that you will need.

Even though this may be a less than pleasant truth, and even though dark psychology is something that many people would rather avoid, it is important to see as something that exists. It is imperative that you see the way that you can navigate through all sorts of relationships that you have so you can and will be able to properly influence others and understand how they can potentially influence you as well. Influence matters and happens constantly, whether you want to admit it or not—it's all a matter of understanding whether it is happening to you or not. It is important to recognize the ways that you can begin to influence others and how you can use those powers for good. You can choose to acknowledge the existence of dark psychology, or you can choose to avoid it and be victimized by it—but either way, it is prevalent.

If you choose to read through this entire series on human psychology, you will see that there is an entire book dedicated to understanding dark psychology. We would go through the various methods that can be used so they can be understood and even utilized yourself if you chose to do so. You can choose to utilize dark psychology, but you must also understand that at the heart of it all is an understanding of psychology in a more general, broader sense that will grant you that power. If you want that power, then keep reading. Pay attention to the ways that the human mind works so you can begin to apply it as well. The more that you do this, the more in control of any situation that you will become. If you want to ace a job interview, you can do it! You just have to understand how the mind of your interviewer works. Do you want to be seen as highly attractive? You can do that as well! All you have to do is tap into how people tend to navigate these situations. This control becomes highly influential to you and grants you that power to be the best person that you can be.

CHAPTER 3: WHAT IS NLP?

Have you ever gone through the effort of trying to communicate with someone else that does not speak the same language as you? Perhaps you speak English, and the other person speaks Chinese. The person speaking Chinese is desperately gesturing for something, but you are entirely unsure what it is that they need. They gesture frantically, but you never figure it out. You make many guesses—you offer a phone, and they shake their head. You offer water, and they shake their head. No matter what you offer, the other person becomes more and more annoyed or frustrated because he or she cannot get through to you. Eventually, the other person storms off without having ever gotten whatever it is that he needed and you are left wondering what it was that was so desperately needed in the first place.

Now, imagine that same exchange, but you are both the English and Chinese speaker—one half of you only speaks in English while the other desperately tries to communicate in Chinese. Neither side is able to communicate with the other, and both end up disjointed, frustrated, and without any proper communication. This is actually what does happen in your mind. Your conscious mind thinks in one way, and the unconscious mind thinks entirely differently. You may want to be setting up a life to be happy and successful, but in reality, your unconscious has never received the message. As a result, you find that your unconscious continuously sabotages you. Your emotions do not line up with your goals. Your body language does not fit. You simply run into complication after complication, despite the fact that you know what you want.

Keep in mind that your unconscious mind is not meant to be your adversary. It is not something that needs to be tamed or controlled. Rather, it is something to harness and work within tandem. However, this means that you need to learn to communicate with it appropriately. If you can figure out the right way to communicate with that unconscious part of yourself, you *can* get it lined up with your conscious desires and expectations. You *can* get it to help you achieve your goals. It is not a matter of your unconscious being out to get you or subvert your attempts to happiness; it is a matter of you do not know how best to communicate with your unconscious mind to get what you want.

Neuro-Linguistic Programming

This is where neuro-linguistic programming comes in. NLP is designed to help you facilitate getting the results that you want and need. It helps you figure out how best to act in ways that are conducive to your success. Those who practice NLP say that the unconscious mind is what drives you to achieve your goals, so long as you are able to communicate those goals effectively. NLP recognizes that both the conscious and unconscious minds are important and serve their own roles.

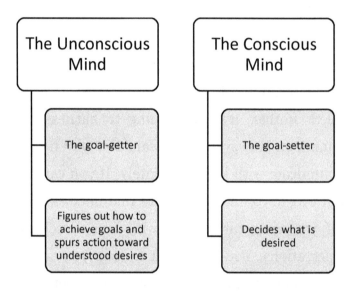

NLP helps to bridge that gap between the two, acting as a sort of translator, so your conscious desires are communicated to the unconscious mind in order to ensure that your mind works together rather than against each other. By working together, you will find that you are far more likely to see your desired results simply because you are not running into the problem of having the two parts of your mind clash.

Effectively, neuro-linguistic processing is a method of learning to communicate with the unconscious. You are learning to become fluent in your unconscious mind's method of communication so you can finally tell it what you want. It allows for that communication with yourself, but also facilitates the communication with others as well. This means that you can use the processes learned during the practice of NLP to also communicate with the unconscious minds of others as well. You can implant thoughts, facilitate behaviors, and encourage changes in lifestyles all by learning how to tap into the unconscious minds of others.

While this may sound manipulative, you actually see people paying others to give them the NLP treatment. People will pay practitioners to help them overcome phobias or bad habits. People can be taught to overcome emotions, create new coping methods, and more all by interacting with someone fluent in NLP.

For example, imagine that you have severe anxiety because, as a child, you went up to present something, but you really needed to use the bathroom. You could not go before the presentation, and as you gave it, you accidentally had an accident. Everyone laughed at you, and ever since, you have been *terrified* of ever getting involved in presentations. Being in front of a crowd became something that you could not possibly bring yourself to do. You failed several assignments all through school because you simply would refuse to present. You would do the work, but you would not go up to present it.

Obviously, there are plenty of job choices during which you would never have to be in front of a crowd, but if you happened to choose a job that would regularly put you in front of people to deliver reports, you may find that you struggle. You know that you are not a child anymore and that realistically, you would not be wetting yourself again any time soon, but you cannot get over that feeling of being laughed at and horrified.

As a solution, you may have spoken to an NLP practitioner. The practitioner would have access to several tools that could help you process that trauma in order to get past it. You could reframe the situation, learning to laugh at it instead of feeling traumatized. You could learn to create anchors that will have you begin to feel an entirely different feeling when you go up to present. No matter the method, there are several tools that can be used to help you get over that trauma.

This is just one example of a time that NLP can be used to benefit. However, it can also be used in ways that are harmful. Manipulators love the tools of NLP because they grant access to the unconscious mind. The manipulator can use NLP techniques to create tendencies to obey almost mindlessly. They can create tendencies to give the manipulator exactly what he or she wants. The manipulator will be able to communicate with the unconscious mind without ever tripping the alarms of the conscious mind. Effectively, the manipulator is able to completely bypass the conscious and tell the unconscious exactly what is expected— and the unconscious will comply. Without any clear way to communicate, the individual will be left frustrated, wondering why they keep behaving the way that they are with no clear answer.

The Keys to NLP

For NLP to be effective, there are a few steps that need to be followed. These are the keys to NLP that will help you figure out how to access the mind. At this point, you are being shown a brief overview of what needs to happen. There are techniques that will more or less use these steps on their own and other steps that will seek to change things up a bit. However, at the heart of things, these must happen. These three steps, the keys to being able to practice NLP, are being able to examine and identify beliefs, choosing an appropriate anchor, and then setting that anchor in an efficient manner.

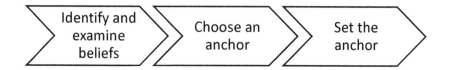

If you can master these three simple steps, you will find that the more specific techniques seem to fall into place with ease. You will be able to convince people to do almost anything, simply by knowing how to get into the other person's mind. This is a strategic endeavor, but once you are able to follow that strategy, you will find that the control that you can exert over both yourself and others around you is far more than you had access to ever before. You will become the master over your own behavior, while also having the power and access to other people to be a master over them as well. You can effectively use these NLP techniques and strategies to figure out how best to win the long game.

Examine beliefs

First, you are figuring out the information at hand. This is where you start to piece together what you or the other person think or feel surrounding a certain event or situation. You may find that the other person is highly anxious about socializing and being in front of crowds. When in front of a crowd, they tend to melt down and freak out. You know this and acknowledge it.

You will be examining beliefs to figure out *why* that is felt. In this case, it may link back to that one incident of wetting herself in front of a crowd and then being mortified any time she is under public scrutiny.

If you are attempting to use NLP on yourself, which is a valid technique that many people will use, you may take this time to identify the emotion that you have that you wish was not problematic. You may figure out that you tend to feel angry during certain situations, and because of that anger, you struggle to really communicate with other people effectively. That lack of communication usually has the unfortunate result of causing problems in your relationships.

As you identify those feelings, you will find that you can figure out where the problem lies. In figuring them out, you can start to figure out how best to target and destroy them. In NLP, this process usually involves the use of anchors—points that are directly related to a certain event or feeling. An anchor for your stress, for example, maybe you bite your nails out of habit, but after a lifetime of biting your nails when stress, just the act of absently biting your nails can make your anxiety begin to flare up.

Choose an anchor

Knowing that you will be under the influence of several anchors already, certain situations or actions that cause you to feel a certain emotion, it is time to figure out which anchors and emotions you can use to overcome the problem. If you know that you have an anger issue, you may go through the effort of learning how to combat that anger issue through triggering new emotions instead. Whenever you would feel yourself getting angry, then you would make sure that you trigger your anchor, and that would then cause you to feel something else.

Effectively, if you are familiar with basic psychology, you are conditioning yourself. You are effectively training yourself to act a certain way in response to certain situations, and in doing so, you are able to make sure that you can overcome the negative feelings that have been holding you down. If you have bad habits in relation to your emotions, you can begin to counter them. You can figure out how to create new, healthier habits that trigger you to behave in new, healthier ways. You can figure out how best to protect yourself from your negative emotions so you can heal and move on in life.

Your new anchor can be just about anything. You could use an affirmation or word that you repeat to yourself to help keep yourself under control. It could be a movement or an action that you use to remind yourself to stay under control, such as snapping your wrist with a rubber band whenever you find that your anger is getting out of hand. It could be a scent that makes you feel secure. It can even be a certain thought or memory that you return to during times of distress.

When you choose an anchor, you want to make sure that it is something that you can regularly access for maximum impact. You may be best served with a short phrase that you use or a motion of your hands. That is something that you can do subtly and at any point in time.

Set an anchor

Finally, you must figure out how to set your anchor. This is where you see the most deviation in your behaviors and techniques. There are several different methods that can be used in order to set a good anchor point for you or for those around you, and how you decide to do so will largely be dependent upon what you are hoping to do and how you are dealing with. You may choose to use visualization if you are working with someone intentionally, with the other person knowing what you are doing. You may choose to use something more along the lines of mirroring and subtle mimicry and emotional triggers if you want to be entirely unnoticed. You may choose to do something like intentionally reframing a memory from negative and traumatic into something funny if you want to change your own way of thinking and your own emotional reaction. Ultimately, the method that you choose will largely be subject to who you are attempting to persuade and how you want to go about it.

If you want to make it a point to, for example, persuade a stranger to buy something that you want them to, you may make it a point to trigger a mirroring relationship—do not worry if you do not know how to do this. It will be discussed in Chapter 8. From there, you can subtly influence him to nod his head by nodding your own head, making the other person's mindset far more likely to be agreeable, and leading to the other person being influenced to nod along with you without ever realizing that you had influenced and encouraged that decision.

Whether you want to control yourself or someone else, you always want to choose an anchor that is simple and easily implemented, but not so common that it will be randomly triggered by strangers during the course of the day. While you probably could trigger someone to make a certain face every time you do a very specific and common movement, such as giving a thumbs up, it would not be particularly kind or ethical to do so. You would be triggering the other person in a way that will likely be distracting and problematic. After all, no one wants to be grimaced at every time they give a thumbs up to someone else.

The History of NLP

NLP, like nearly any psychological technique, has changed drastically from creation to what you now know and see today. While the root is still the same, there are different ways that the thoughts and techniques are approached now compared to what was seen back when it was first founded in the 1970s. This chapter will provide you with a brief overview of how NLP has changed and what you can expect if you were to use NLP today. Ultimately, you can think of NLP as what it was during creation and within the four waves of NLP.

The Creation of NLP

Created in 1972 by two psychotherapists named Richard Bandler and John Grinder, this process was originally designed to model several other therapeutic processes at the time. In particular, it referenced and developed from techniques such as gestalt therapy, hypnotherapy, and systemic family therapy. All of these came together to create an approach that would address two specific things: Why are psychotherapists special or skilled in influencing others? How can that specialty be transferred to other normal people without any formal training in psychology?

These two thoughts then triggered the beginning of the development of NLP. IN particular, people were taught to look at each of the aforementioned psychotherapy processes. Bandler and Grinder drew from those different forms of psychotherapy and pulled out any processes or techniques that they thought were critical in making the therapist so powerful. They identified the patters in communication and attitudes and were able to then create and build a list of techniques and beliefs drawing from those forms of psychotherapy. Thus, NLP was born.

NLP as primarily existed within four specific waves, during which different aspects were focused on or developed. These four waves are important to understand in order to truly understand what NLP was and what it has become.

- **Wave 1: NLPure:** In the first wave of NLP, you see the original NLP as developed by Bandler and Grinder. This is the purest form, during which success and enthusiasm were the most important factors that were pushed.
- **Wave 2: NLPt:** In the second wave, you see NLP used as an application in psychotherapy. It is commonly referred to as neuro-linguistic psychotherapy, and it began in 1989. This was all

about making sure that people had a healthy and happy approach and view of life.

- **Wave 3: NLPeace:** This third wave, NLPeace, arose in 1992, with a focus on spirituality. Instead of focusing on how to fix the mind itself, it was focusing on how to find meaning in life and figure out how to connect spiritually.

- **Wave 4: NLPsy:** Finally, the fourth wave encompasses the use of neuro-linguistic processing as a form of psychology. Beginning in 2006, this was used to being to identify psychological patterns. It requires a master's degree in psychology, for a qualification to practice psychotherapy, and also an NLP master training qualification. Effectively, when you see someone that practices NLPsy, you know that they have gone through years of schooling in order to be as effective as possible when it comes to offering treatment.

When you seek out NLP treatment from a professional, you will likely face someone that is trained in fourth wave NLP. This is good—they are licensed to help you and can enable you to be the healthiest you that you can be. However, remember that NLP itself was designed to be accessible even to the average person. While you are not qualified to diagnose people if you have not gone to school to become licensed to do so, you will still be able to develop an affinity for several NLP processes so you can use them effectively and in ways that you know are beneficial to others around you or to yourself.

CHAPTER 4: NLP BASIC PRINCIPLES TO IMPROVE LIFE

Before really delving into the processes of NLP and how you can utilize them, it is important to recognize that there are several principles that you will have to keep in mind. When you want to use NLP, you must meet these principles if you want to be able to be successful. After all, accessing other people's unconscious minds will require you to be patient, flexible, and willing to spend the time to do so effectively. You will need to have a clear plan ready for yourself so you can actively address and live by the rules that you are seeking to make use of.

Think of these as your guiding processes that will help you to make sure that you are able to use NLP. These will be your founding principles that you will live by if you want to be able to tap into the unconscious. These will guide you in being successful, whether you want to improve your own life or convince someone else to do something specific. No matter what you choose to do, you will be able to do so, if you keep these steps in mind.

In particular, the steps that will be addressed here are being able to know your outcome, take action, maintain sensory acuity, have flexibility, and live by a physiology of excellence. With these five principles, NLP will be successful for you. This chapter will guide you through learning how to utilize these principles in your own life. You will be able to help yourself. You will be able to help others. Above all, you will be able to be effective and successful.

Know your outcome

The first and most important place to start when you are attempting to live with the utilization of NLP is knowing your outcome. This is effectively figuring out exactly what you want, how you will get it, and why you want it. If you do not know what the outcome you want is, how can you possibly hope to ever achieve it? If you do not know that you want to be a lawyer, for example, can you possibly reasonably expect yourself to go through law school and build up all that debt, only to find out after the fact that law was your passion after all? No—no one in their right mind would ever put themselves through law school without ever knowing that they wanted to be a lawyer or that their true goal in life was to be a lawyer. People may go through law school because they have been told their whole life that they should go to law school, but even those people grew up with the expectation of being a lawyer. No one goes to law school without the expectation or desire to become that person.

Just like no one would ever expect that you must know your own outcome and desires if you want to succeed. You need to figure out exactly what you want in life so you can figure out how to get it. Do you want to be rich? Do you want to find love? Maybe you want to be a parent, or you want to become a firefighter. No matter what the dream is, you need to know and vocalize it to yourself if you want it to become a reality. If you want to be rich, you can tell yourself that. If you want to be happy, you can tell yourself that, too. What your goal is in life is not as important as knowing what that goal is. That knowledge is power and will help you during your process.

If you are using NLP for other people, you may want to know what your end goal for that person is. Do you want them to be happy? Do you want them to buy that car you are selling? Maybe you want them to break up with their narcissistic partner. No matter what it is you want, you need to know what it is if you hope to make it happen.

Once you know what you want, it is time to form it in a way that you can act upon it. This is effectively just coming up with a way to structure your desires so you can act upon them. When you do this, you must meet certain specific criteria to ensure that the outcome is well-formed. This is a fancy way of saying that if you want your goal to be actionable and attainable, you need to word it in the proper manner. These criteria are critical to making sure that you are able to act accordingly. These criteria are:

- **Positive-oriented:** Your goal must be focused on what you *do* want, not what you would like to avoid. For example, you must state that you want to find love, versus you don't want to be alone any longer. Shifting this to a positive instead of a negative gives you something to work toward instead of something to avoid.

- **Sensory specific:** As we continue along the NLP path, you will begin to see that every method of influence on someone else, whether it is on yourself or on someone else, is sensory. You must figure out which senses you will be targeting and how those senses will perceive when you have been successful at achieving your goal. Perhaps this will be that you can see that you have a partner if your end goal is to find love. If you want to sell that car, perhaps you decide that the sensory input will be having the paperwork with the signatures in your hand. Try to address how each of your five senses will interact with the outcome when it has been achieved. This helps you be able to truly visualize what you want.

- **Contextual:** This involves making sure that you know the context under which you will be successful. You are acknowledging what has to happen if you want to be successful. Where will it happen? When? How? Who will you be with? When you know the context of what you are seeking, you will be able to acknowledge what you need to do to set up the environment properly to ensure that you do happen to get whatever you are hoping to achieve.

- **Self-achievable:** You must make sure that the goal you want is one that you can set into action on your own without the influence of other people. You may need to make sure that other people are doing something, but can you do so? You must have access to the resources that you will need to achieve your goal.

- **Ecological:** This is as simple as asking three specific questions for yourself: Is it good for you? Is it good for other people? Is it for the greater good? Remember, NLP is all about bettering the world and those who are using it. While it is often used as a tool for manipulation and controlling others, that is not always the intention.

- **Worthwhile:** Finally, you must make sure that whatever the outcome that you are trying to achieve is worthwhile. Is it something that will actually be useful and positive to you? It does not have to be useful on a daily basis, but you should be able to see some good from whatever it is. You may have enhanced other people's lives, allowing your friend to no longer be terrified of crowds, which indirectly improves your own life because your friend is happier and healthier. On the other hand, you may directly address a problem of your own in an attempt to better yourself, and that is okay too. So long as it is effective, either directly or indirectly, it is good enough.

Take action

The next step to making sure that you are able to be successful in using NLP is to take action. This is something that may seem like common sense, but many people entirely miss this step altogether. You must be willing to act if you hope to see any results. If you want to ensure that you can actually change your life or change the behaviors of someone else, you must figure out reasons to work or do something.

Oftentimes, people fall into the trap of inaction—they feel like they cannot possibly succeed, and therefore they fall victim to procrastination. However, this is your mind's attempt to avoid action in order to protect yourself from failure. When you protect yourself in this way, it is easy to make excuses and act like it happened for a reason- you may tell yourself that you are too dumb to really make a difference, or that you will fail even if you try.

Well, guess what: Failure happens. People fail all the time, but that is not inherently bad. When you fail, you learn. When you learn, you become better prepared for your next attempt. It is okay to fail, so long as you learn from that failure and do not let it define you. Effectively, then, you want to live through learning from that failure and not letting the fear of failure keep you locked in inaction.

When you are practicing NLP, you *must* act. If you refuse to act, nothing gets done. Nothing changes. People's behaviors remain the same. You fail. NLP is not passive—it requires constant action and effort, and for that reason, you must be willing to go through the motions and make whatever it is that you want happen.

Sensory acuity

Next, you must learn sensory acuity. This is effectively learning to cue into all of the important body language that you will need to understand if you hope to be able to use NLP. NLP is all about being able to look at someone else, understand their mindset and processes, and then use those processes in order to figure out how to influence the other person's mind as well.

Stop and consider for a moment what body language is—it is unconscious movements that are designed to convey very specific meanings. Your unconscious mind is largely responsible for your body language—if you are anxious, your body language will convey that. If you are happy, your body language will convey that. This means that if you learn how to read the body language of someone else, you will be able to read the state of their unconscious mind.

This is because body language and actions are directly influenced by thoughts. They exist within a cycle—thoughts influence feelings and those feelings influence behavior. Effectively, then, you can learn to track the thoughts by learning to identify behavior. You can also take this one step further by learning to change thoughts by influencing behavior as well.

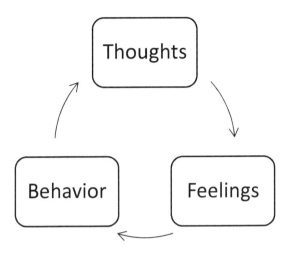

Effectively, then, sensory acuity is the ability to focus entirely externally. Think about what happens most of the time when someone is telling you a story. If you are not trained in effective listening, you may make it a point to constantly be coming up with arguments that you can use to make a certain point in response. You may feel like you are listening, but in reality, your mind is also busy trying to come up with some sort of reaction or counterargument. This is problematic— you are not paying close enough attention to the other party, and you run some serious risks in doing so. However, you can learn to defeat this. You can learn to focus entirely on listening instead.

When you focus on sensory acuity, focusing on what the other person is doing as they talk, you are paying complete attention. You see all of those minute shifts in body language. You are seeing the other person change up what they are doing in response to you. You are seeing those subtle signs that may betray a lie, or that say that the other person is uncomfortable with the line of questioning but is desperate to try to remain open in communication.

Effectively, then, you must learn to always listen attentively. You must learn how to recognize these aspects of body language so you can use them as feedback for yourself. In learning to recognize that body language, you can effectively allow yourself to respond appropriately, or to glean all of that information that you will need in order to be successful with the attempts to persuade with NLP.

Behavioral Flexibility

Another important aspect of NLP is flexibility. NLP is not an exact science simply because no two people are the same. People are complex, and so too are their minds. One person may be entirely comfortable with talking about a personal issue while the other is terrified to mention similar issues. You may find that some people are happy to comply without resistance, and others are completely unresponsive to your best attempts to influence. Because no two minds are the same, you must be willing to engage in a little trial and error. You cannot simply decide that you will come up with a one size fits all approach to accessing other people's minds—you must be willing to entertain several different possibilities and to change things up when you hit a roadblock.

Oftentimes, people fail at this—they simply stubbornly refuse to ever engage in anything other than what they have originally set out to do, but the results never change. If it failed the first and second time, why do you think that the same attempt would pass the next time? If you never try anything different, the change will never arrive. You need to be able to focus on change if you want to be successful at NLP. You need to be flexible in your own behaviors. You need to be flexible in what you are willing to try.

This helps beyond just learning NLP, too—when you use this, you are effectively making yourself more flexible in general. You are teaching yourself to cope with failure or the unexpected with ease. You will no longer be afraid of failing or feeling like you cannot try anything else. It helps you become more likely to succeed simply because you are willing to step out of your comfort zone and mix things up when you need to. If you are unwilling to make concessions or change your best attempts at dealing with a situation, all you are going to do is keep yourself stubbornly rooted in failure and control rather than looking at things as being a chance for improvement.

Physiology of excellence

Finally, if you want to be successful in your endeavors with NLP, you must be able to operate from a position of health. You need to be feeling physically and mentally sound if you hope to operate at your best, which means that you must be able to take care of yourself. You cannot take care of others if you cannot take care of yourself, so you must be willing to maintain that physiology of excellence.

Just as you are told that you must put your own oxygen mask on before tending to your children on an airplane, you must be willing to take care of yourself before you are willing to take on the world's problems. You need to ensure that you are healthy. This means that you must engage in self-care. You must make sure that you are healthy. You must make sure that you get the proper rest to maintain yourself.

In particular, if you find that your life is not giving you the excellence that you need or that you are not as healthy as you could be, you should put in the time to achieve it. You may need to use some of your own NLP techniques to achieve this, such as teaching yourself to be more diligent about your own sleep or exercise regimen or reminding yourself to eat healthily. However, you owe it to yourself and to those around you that are relying on you to keep yourself healthy. After all, you cannot possibly focus on the other person if you are not feeling well.

Besides just being in your own best interest, if you are able to make sure that you are healthy, you will rub off on those that you are with. If you adopt your own healthy lifestyle, those closest to you are more likely to begin to adapt some of those tendencies for themselves as well.

CHAPTER 5: NLP MIND CONTROL

Have you ever interacted with someone before and found that, inexplicably, you were beginning to have strange and powerful temptations about what to do next? Perhaps you felt like you needed to do something that you would ordinarily never bother with, or you find that your emotions seem to be strangely all over the place, despite the fact that you should have been able to manage them well enough.

There may be an explanation for this: Neuro-Linguistic processing. This is a particularly powerful set of actions. Words, and behaviors in order to trigger other people into obedience. Effectively, you will be able to access and interact with the other person's mind, quietly and subtly controlling their mind in ways that were likely entirely unexpected.

NLP practitioners vary from people genuinely interested in helping someone else in the world out to people with no other intention but to manipulate and harm others. In particular, these techniques are incredibly difficult to identify, and in not being able to figure them out, you may find that more and more of your behavior changes over time. For that reason, it is incredibly critical that you develop the ability to understand exactly what NLP is and how it works. Not only will you be able to wield these tools yourself if you so choose, you will also be able to identify ways that the usage of these behaviors can be beneficial to everyone

What is Neuro-Linguistic Processing?

Ultimately, NLP is the ability to learn how to communicate effectively with the unconscious mind of either yourself or of others. When you can access the unconscious mind of someone else, you are effectively learning to bypass all of the checks and balances in place to ensure that they are able to retain free will. In particular, you are learning to become a translator between the conscious and unconscious minds. The conscious and unconscious mind both really struggle to interact meaningfully with each other—one wants one thing, but the other cannot quite understand the request. In the end, wires seem to get crossed, and no one is happy with what has happened, how it happened, or what ends up being the end result.

However, with NLP, you can learn to speak that language of the unconscious mind. NLP looks to identify the ways that you can do just that in order to make sure that the unconscious mind is actively communicated with in ways that are meaningful and important. This means that you will be able to ensure that the conscious and unconscious mind are working in tandem with each other.

This is important because, as is commonly said in NLP, the conscious mind works out the actions and what is wanted while the unconscious mind is tasked with ensuring that the goals and actions actually happen.

Stop and think about what the unconscious mind does for a moment—it is responsible for taking care of any and all automatic actions throughout the day. You do not think about driving—your unconscious mind does it for you. You do not think about how to brush your teeth—your unconscious does that too. Basically, your unconscious mind goes through all of the motions, making sure that you are doing exactly what you need to get through your day with the least amount of effort possible. It wants to reserve valuable conscious mind real estate for issues that are actually important, such as making an important decision on which job to apply for or how to go about achieving that difficult goal that you have planned out. Because there is only so much that can be fit into the conscious mind, the unconscious takes over for you. It allows you to run on autopilot for all of those tedious actions that you must get through during the course of your day. Without the unconscious mind, you would find that you need to decide and consciously focus on brushing your teeth, buckling up, and more.

NLP to Control Minds

If the unconscious mind is what takes care of all of your automatic, habitual behaviors, then, you may wonder why that is what NLP seeks to target. This is a great question—and there is a very simple answer. The unconscious mind is responsible for emotions. Emotions are unconscious reactions to the world around you. You do not choose to feel happiness or anger; it just happens. However, emotions are incredibly motivating.

Your thoughts that underlie everything influence those emotions. Your emotions then influence your behaviors. If you want to control behaviors, you want to be able to alter emotions, and it just so happens to be that the easiest way to alter emotions is through figuring out how to directly tap into the thoughts of someone else.

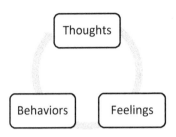

When you tap into the unconscious mind, then, you are able to mess around with that sequence. You can figure out how to create new thoughts, feelings, and behaviors, all because you are bypassing the conscious mind and interacting with the unconscious. Since the unconscious will almost never actually be acknowledged by the conscious in the moment, this is the best way to directly and simply interact with the other person to avoid raising red flags.

When you use NLP, you are using a process that has been used for years primarily in a therapeutic sense. Despite the popularity of it in recent years when used in tandem with dark psychology and attempts to control people, it was initially designed to be something that could be used regularly to ensure that people were taken care of and healthy. It was meant to give power back to the people, looking at what makes psychologists so qualified to help other people when regular people are not. Effectively, NLP techniques are ways to grant the powers of a psychologist to normal people with little training. These techniques can then be used in ways that will benefit everyone involved—you will be able to actively help other people with ease. You will be able to alleviate doubt, create anchors to instill confidence, and more, all because you have these skills.

Of course, there is still the possibility of using this mind control for more nefarious reasons. Just as simply as you could use these techniques in order to help other people, you can use them specifically to hurt others as well. Instead of alleviating anxiety or traumatic memories, you can make associations with fear and avoidance in order to push someone further under your thumb.

Effectively, when you learn how to use NLP, you hold the mind of someone else, their entire being, in the palm of your hand, and you will be able to manipulate it at will.

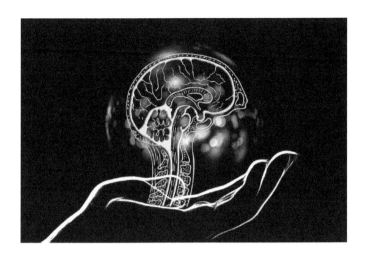

NLP and Mirroring

Ultimately, before you can do anything with NLP, you must become a well-liked individual. You must be able to develop what is known as rapport with the person that you are attempting to influence, as without that rapport, you have no entrance into the other person's unconscious.

Your rapport with someone is effectively an accurate measure of just how likely you are to be persuasive with that individual. If you want to be able to impact the other person's mind, you need to be able to access it, and the best way to access it is to lower the other person's guard.

Before understanding how to create that rapport, however, consider that the unconscious mind is always watching. Even if your conscious mind cannot possibly process everything that you are being exposed to, your unconscious mind is still able to pick up on things. It recognizes even subliminal signals, such as those included in advertisement that completely subvert conscious understanding—and that subversion is what makes this process so powerful. When you can subvert someone else's mind, you can take control of it.

Mirroring is just one way of creating that rapport and gaining access. When you mirror someone, you are telling them something specific—that they matter to you and that you feel some sort of connection to them. Mirroring is what people naturally do as they grow to know those around them better. Look at two best friends for a few minutes and you will see it—they will both walk the same, talk the same, take drinks nearly in tandem with each other, and more. They do this all for a simple reason: Their unconscious minds have developed that rapport with each other. They are directly communicating with the unconscious mind of the other person, saying that they do like and appreciate that other person, and that the other person has their utmost trust.

While developing a natural relationship will always be the best way to create rapport, you do not always have time for that. In those instances, you can create rapport with three simple steps: Create a connection, match the other person, and then identify their punctuator.

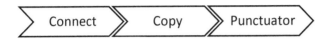

Creating that initial connection is not particularly difficult— you will want to make good, convincing eye contact, spend the time to listen to the other person, and will the connection into existence. You effectively want to give the other person your utmost, undivided attention in hopes of them realizing that you do enjoy what they are talking about. During this stage, try giving the occasional triple nod. This is when you nod three times in a row, usually pensively, to communicate three things to the other person's unconscious mind. You will tell them that you are attentive, understanding, and agreeing with the other person.

With that initial connection created, you will then make it a point to copy the other person. In particular, you may find that the best way to do this is through copying their vocal cues. While body language is always an easy target to mimic, you also risk raising red flags simply because you are mimicking them, and people generally do not appreciate when someone else is copying them. Instead, concentrate on their verbal cues.

When you do this, you will usually start by matching the speaking speed and intensity of the other person. If they want to speak to you animatedly, return that right back to them. If they are speaking to you calmly and quietly, you should do the same. In doing so, you are letting them know that you are on the same page as them, even if the behaviors do not necessarily line up quite right. Nevertheless, it is important.

With the verbal cues mimicked, try figuring out what the other person's punctuator is. The punctuator is something that all people do in emphasis when they are talking. Some people may have a saying that they use immediately after making the point that they want to emphasize while other people may intentionally raise their eyebrows or make a movement of the hand. What is true either way is that the punctuator is something that the other person will have, and if you can identify it, you can use it.

Once it is identified, you should make it a point to actively use it. The next time that you think the other person is likely to use the punctuator, mimic it. In mimicking it, you will tell the other person's unconscious mind that you are someone that can be related to, and thus, you open up their mind.

Of course, you will want to test that connection before moving forward—you want to ensure that the connection made is valid before you go attempting to use NLP in other ways. All you need to do is move a certain way to determine if the other person will move like you do. If they do, you were successful. If not, then you have likely run into some sort of snag and they are not going to be as likely to follow along.

NLP to Create Anchors

After creating that rapport, one of the simplest NLP techniques that you can use when interacting with someone else is to create anchors. Anchors are effectively a form of conditioning that can be wielded in order to control the behaviors of someone else. Think about how Pavlov's dogs were taught to respond to the bell with salivating even if food is not around—that is exactly what you are doing when you anchor someone, except you are most likely using a technique that is far less humiliating.

When you want to start out, you must have a rapport built with the other party. With that rapport built, you will want to ensure that you can actively interact with the other person regularly. Since you will effectively be conditioning the other person, you need to be able to do it with the freedom to trigger and expose the other person.

Anchoring effectively requires you to follow a few simple steps: You will need to figure out what the anchoring feeling that you want to use is. Then you must identify a way for you to trigger that feeling. From there, you must choose your anchor. With the anchor determined, you will need to trigger the feeling with the chosen trigger, and then simultaneously use the anchor at the same time. Over time of having the feeling and anchor coincide together on a regular basis, the other person will, eventually, become anchored—that is to say, the anchor will trigger the feeling that you wanted to pair with it.

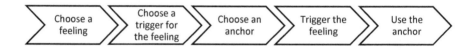

This process is actually far simpler than it sounds. For example, imagine that you want to anchor your friend that has anxiety. He is always stressing out about finals when he has them coming up, and as a college student, those finals come up regularly. This means that he has no choice but to face that fear regularly.

You decide that you would rather figure out how to alleviate that anxiety with something relatively simple. You decide that you want to teach him to feel relaxed when he is exposed to the scratching sound of a pencil. After all, during a final, he is likely to hear the constant scratching of pencils on paper.

Now, you have chosen a feeling and an anchor. What you missed, however, was the trigger for that feeling. Perhaps you remember that your friend is always super relaxed when he is listening to music. Something about it soothes his soul, he always says. You then play the music as you are sitting next to him and begin scratching away at some paper. You may actually be writing, doodling, or literally just scribbling in circles, but the end result is him beginning to relax as he listens to the music.

You repeat this process over time, making sure that it happens regularly as you want to ensure that you really install that conditioning well. After a few weeks, you find that just scribbling on your paper does, in fact, help him calm down, which then enables you to trigger that calmness at will.

He never realizes what you did, but right around the next final, he tells you that he is feeling strangely confident as he goes in—that he feels like he is well prepared because as he had studied and took notes, he found himself incredibly calm instead of freaking out like he normally is.

NLP and Pace and Lead

Similar to being able to anchor someone, another technique you can use after being able to mirror and set up that valuable rapport with someone else is the ability to pace and lead. When you can pace and lead, you are effectively able to control the emotional state of someone else with two simple steps: You first match what they are doing, and then you change the tempo or intensity of it.

Remember, mirroring is usually a mutual occurrence—when you are mirroring someone else, they are far more likely to mirror you as well, and you need to remember to use that concept to your own advantage. When you are mirroring someone else, then, and you can see them mirroring you, you can begin to tap into their body language with your own. This means that you can gently and quietly guide them into doing something else without them ever actively thinking about it.

For example, imagine that you are talking to that same nervous friend. This time, he is terrified because he wants to ask someone else on a date, but he is too afraid to do it. He is nervously tapping his fingers against the table and shifting back and forth, clear signs of his current anxiety. Instead of leaving him to it without attempting to help, however, you stop and begin to tap your finger on your hand subtly as you listen. You do not make it a point to make it obvious, but you allow it to happen at the same pace as your friend's. After a bit, you slowly begin to slow down the speed that you are tapping, and you shift your own body language to being relaxed and open. You may slow down your own breathing in an attempt to impact his own breathing rate.

After a while, you notice that his tapping is slowing down with yours. This means that your technique is working, and eventually, when you stop tapping your own fingers, you will see that he does, too.

CHAPTER 6: HYPNOSIS

Finally, we have reached hypnosis—of the techniques for mind control that you are learning, this will be the last. As you work toward the ability to hypnotize people, keep in mind everything else that you have learned thus far. The minds of other people are absolutely sacred and should be treated as such. If you are going to be influencing other people, you should always make sure to do it ethically. Remember, just because hypnotizing someone for your own selfish gain is dangerous and not recommended does not mean that hypnosis itself is bad. In fact, hypnosis has gained massive traction lately. You see it used during labor, with women self-hypnotizing themselves in order to avoid the pain of labor, focusing through the contractions as a way to manage their own comfort. You see people using hypnosis for cessation of cigarettes or other unhealthy habits. You even see people using it to help them become more self-confident.

Ultimately, hypnosis has no shortage of usage or of people willing to try it. If you remember to keep your control of other people ethical and consensual, there is no harm in using these methods. However, you must always emphasize consent above all.

Nevertheless, it is time to delve into the mysterious world of hypnosis. Within this chapter, you will learn about how hypnosis works, understanding that it is not the utmost control over other people that is typically depicted in cartoons or movies—instead, it is a state of extreme relaxation and suggestibility. We will go over a few positive uses of hypnosis, such as in labor and delivery, and finally, we will look over the steps on how to hypnotize someone else that is willing to be your subject. If all goes well, you will find that influencing other people is far easier than you may have thought.

How Hypnosis Works

Primarily, hypnosis works because it is cooperative—usually, one person is willingly being relaxed into a hypnotic state, and the hypnotist then encourages the thoughts and behaviors that are desired. In a therapeutic situation, this may look like encouraging the individual to no longer care about an ex that left or being able to resist those cravings of sugar and to exercise more. Effectively, it allows for the implantation of thoughts in a consensual way.

This means that the hypnotist is just the coach—they are there to guide the way through the subconscious to create the results that the individual that is being hypnotized wanted in the first place. The hypnotist effectively is able to manage to walk the individual through the steps of hypnosis, and in doing so, guides the individual to that state of extreme calmness.

Within the hypnotic state, it is often reported that the one being hypnotized is convinced that they are asleep. They are so deeply relaxed that they feel like they are entirely unaware of the world around them. However, that could not be further from the truth—when you are in a hypnotic state, you are actually incredibly aware and focused—but only on what the hypnotist is saying. If the hypnotist is guiding you through breathing practices to keep you calm, all you will focus on is what the hypnotist is saying. If the hypnotist happens to be using any sort of prop or focal object, you will focus on that. In being so incredibly focused on one particular moment or instance, you will find that you are able to be readily and easily influenced.

This primarily works because of the divide between the conscious and unconscious minds. While the two minds work together, the conscious mind acts like a sort of filter between what the unconscious mind is being exposed to and the mind itself. This means that the conscious is basically the guard dog of the mind, and if it interferes, you are not going to be able to get through to the more susceptible, impressionable unconscious, which is where suggestions are meant to go.

When you encourage the conscious mind to focus entirely on one object or action, whether breathing or the swinging of a pendulum, or anything else, you distract the conscious.

Think of what happens if you throw a dog a piece of steak: They run after the steak and happily munch on that while you are free to move forward. Effectively, with hypnosis, you throw your conscious mind a steak by having it so incredibly focused on what is going on.

As this happens, the hypnotist then makes several suggestions. They will talk to the one being hypnotized, making sure that the unconscious mind is able to absorb and internalize all of those thoughts nicely in order to ensure that they do, in fact, become utilized and acted upon. Because the unconscious mind is going to be the one driving actions without the conscious paying attention, those behaviors become quite easy. They simply happen because the unconscious mind does it.

Remember how in NLP, you are actively recognizing that the unconscious mind is the one that controls everything? That is effectively what you are seeing here. Hypnosis, like NLP, will make sure that the unconscious mind is acting accordingly to ensure that the one being hypnotized is able to do what was desired.

Why Use Hypnosis?

Now, with that in mind, you may be wondering why people are so willing and ready to use hypnosis on themselves to the point that they would even pay other people to help them with the process in the first place. The answer is that hypnosis is incredibly powerful because the unconscious is incredibly powerful. It should be used precisely because it does allow people to tap into their unconscious minds to unlock all of the potential that they needed to utilize.

When you use hypnosis, you effectively are making sure that you can draw all of the benefits that your mind has to offer. It offers you benefits such as helping cope with any phobias or anxiety triggers that you may have. If your anxiety and phobia is rooted in your unconscious, what better way to treat it than to directly impact it? It can help with pain management without requiring medication, making it incredibly valuable for people that will need pain medication but may find that they are at an increased risk for addiction or abusing that medication if they have it. It can be used to fight stress as well, working as a sort of grounding method for the individual using it if they want to reach a state of relaxation.

It can also be used in more insidious ways—some people use hypnosis to control other people. It is commonly used in brainwashing in cults, for example, relying on the constant repetition of words or other methods that are designed to tap into the unconscious mind in some way, shape, or form.

This means that hypnosis can be dangerous for those who are particularly susceptible to its effects. Not everyone is, but the vast majority of people are quite susceptible, and this means that these people could be subtly and unknowingly controlled by strangers without ever realizing that it was happening in the first place.

Using Hypnosis

Ultimately, hypnosis happens in several different ways— some people utilize an utter bombardment of the senses in order to trigger that unconscious state, while others will lull people into it with gentle storytelling or guided meditations. Nevertheless, regardless of the method, the end result is the same: The other person ends up being controlled without being aware of it. We will stop and look at two simple methods of hypnosis that can be used to trigger trances, which can then be utilized to ensure that the one being hypnotized is entirely obedient.

Bombardment

Think of a time when you had a teacher or someone else that was extraordinarily boring when they spoke. It didn't matter what was being discussed—their voice was simply so boring;

you could not help but space out when they talked. Though unintentional, that is exactly what this sort of hypnosis accomplishes.

When you use bombardment, you are effectively creating a constant and steady stimulation that drones on to lull the other person into a trance. It could involve someone speaking rapidly in a flat voice or using someone's naturally unvaried voice in order to eventually bore the person into a trance. The brain struggles with processing the information when it is all constant and unending, which is exactly why it becomes so difficult to understand.

If you want to use this, then, you will want to start up a single topic and stick to it for the next several minutes, making your voice as flat as possible. You want to talk as much as possible during that time, not relenting at all, even when you see that the other person is beginning to lose focus. As the focus is lost, you can begin to talk directly to the unconscious mind, making suggestions and encouraging certain behaviors.

Nonverbal Hypnosis

Another method is quite similar but is done in complete silence. However, this one will require you to have rapport built with the individual that you are attempting to hypnotize, as you are going to need to tap into their tendency to mirror you if you want to be effective. When you use this method, you are going to make sure that they are following along with your own body language, and you will start to do something repetitive and rhythmic that is still subtle, expecting the other person to follow suit.

When you use this, you are effectively having the same relaxing effect that you have on an infant that calms down when swayed. Just as the newborn calms down to the motion, so too do adults, even though they may not even realize that they are still susceptible to actions like that.

Start by ensuring that you do have rapport with the other person. With that established, you want to actively mirror the other person for a while until you know that they are mirroring you back. From there, you will begin to use several motions back and forth in an attempt to sway the other person into a relaxed state. However, the key here is making sure that whatever you do, you are making it subtle and easily followed without it seeming to stand out at all when done around other people.

Perhaps you start by tilting your head back and forth ever so slightly. It does not have to be particularly obvious—just gently and subtly move your head in a rhythmic manner.

Chances are, so long as you are subtle enough, the other person will never notice that you are doing it—but they will pick up on it themselves. As you do this, begin to use more of your body as well, but make sure it is still just as subtle. Perhaps you slowly raise and lower your shoulders ever so slightly along with the slight roll of your head. Then, perhaps you also make it a point to rock back and forth on your heels as well. You may also alter your breathing as well in an attempt to ensure that the other person is breathing deeply and calmly.

With some time and effort, you will find that the other person is following all of your cues, especially if you are a trusted party in the first place. As they begin to relax, you will find that they are far more susceptible to what you are saying, and you are more likely to be able to get them to internalize information in this state than before. Make sure that you tell them everything that you wanted their unconscious mind to know before you stop the hypnotic motions, otherwise you risk them coming out of the trance too early, mitigating everything that you are doing.

CHAPTER 7: THE BENEFITS OF DARK PSYCHOLOGY

At last, we arrive at the end of the book, and as we arrive here, it seems fitting to stop with a brief address of reasons that you could use dark psychology in ways that are not nearly as insidious as many that were discussed within the book. Remember, while dark psychology may be based upon looking at how the dark personality types prey on people, that is not all that it is good for—it is incredibly important to understand these abilities and skills. In understanding comes the ability to protect and prevent, after all.

Nevertheless, as you have been exposed to several malicious usages from several of these techniques, let's go over the ethics of dark psychology, as well as the benefits that may arise from it. Dark psychology does not have to be the harmful concept that it has become because of the people that wielded it—you can reclaim it.

Is Dark Psychology Evil?

For the million-dollar question: Is dark psychology evil? The short answer is, no. It is actually neutral. It does not have the capability of being good or evil in the same sense that gravity cannot be good or evil—it simply is. As a force without free will, without any way to control itself, it cannot possibly be labeled with a human construct such as good or evil. However, that does not mean that it is necessarily safe, nor does it mean that it cannot be used in hurtful manners.

While dark psychology itself is not evil, it can be used by evil people. Just as it is not about the gun being evil, but rather the one wielding the gun that determines how evil the situation is, dark psychology is entirely at the mercy of those wielding it. If the individual who uses these techniques uses it for evil purposes, taking advantage of these techniques to steal and abuse, that is his own failure, and no one else's. That failure is something that he will have to address for himself and no one else, and that is significant.

Of course, that means that the inverse is true as well—it cannot truly be a good force either. While dark psychology may not truly be good, it can be used in ways that are beneficial to people, and throughout the book, you were exposed to several. Is it really bad to influence someone to buy a car that will truly better serve their own family? Is it bad to influence someone to no longer have crippling anxiety at the idea of taking a final exam? What about in hypnotizing someone to no longer have insomnia? You would be hard-pressed to find anyone who would claim that any of those were bad decisions or wrong, even though they all used techniques common to dark psychology.

Remember, as dark psychology has been studied, people have gained access into the minds of predators that are capable of far more than the average person is. The average person is not going to be intentionally manipulating and harassing people on the regular—he is going to be minding his own business. He does not have any interest in preying on other people. So, would that average person have a use for dark psychology? Quite possibly! It can be used in ways that were discussed throughout this book, and those can be beneficial to literally anyone that interacts with other people. Several other techniques can be used on yourself as well. You can anchor yourself to create your own coping mechanisms, for example, or you can choose to self-hypnotize in order to help yourself build self-confidence. These are not evil.

Ultimately, whether the art is good or evil, one thing remains true—it is all about how it is used that determines how welcome the use of it is.

Reasons to Use Dark Psychology

There are several reasons that one may intentionally learn dark psychology. They may want to use these methods to help themselves—perhaps they were a victim of a dark personality type in the past and they want to understand why. That insight is invaluable, and gaining the reasons why and how someone was able to entirely and utterly dismantle someone's personality can be therapeutic in some way. In understanding how you have become vulnerable, you can remove those vulnerabilities to figure out how best to fight them off.

Some people may learn about dark psychology out of sheer curiosity—we are fascinated by what scares us. After all, horror is a massive genre in movies for a reason! You may find that learning how the insides of an evil individual's mind works is just as fascinating as it is terrifying, and for that reason alone, you want to keep reading on how they do what they do.

Other people may read simply because they want to be able to fight back. When you can recognize dark psychology, you can prevent it from being effective. So much of dark psychology is all about being able to identify vulnerabilities and exploit them, and if you know those vulnerabilities and about the common exploits, you can simply side-step them. You can avoid falling for them and instead work on strengthening your own skills to protect yourself.

Effectively, dark psychology is incredibly flexible, as are the techniques. The very same techniques that can utterly destroy someone else can also be used in ways that actually better everyone involved. They can build self-confidence and self-esteem. They can help cope with anxiety and other mental health issues. They can make you more likely to be successful in interacting with other people simply because you will have a better understanding.

Above all, you will be able to protect yourself with ease. You will be able to have peace of mind, thanks to learning about dark psychology. At the very least, you will be able to rest easy knowing that the dark personality types will be far less likely to pull a fast one over you simply because you know what to expect.

The Insight of Dark Psychology

Now, as this book finally comes to an end, try to think about the ways that dark psychology and the secrets that it holds may have provided you with insight. What have you learned about the world that you did not know before? What do you know about the mind and how it works? What secrets have you learned that are invaluable?

Dark psychology is quite unique in the sense that it opens the window for us to see through the eyes of the narcissist, the Machiavellian, or the psychopath. In understanding how these techniques work, you can see exactly what spurs these people to act in the ways that they do. You can figure out why people want to behave these ways and what they stand to gain by doing so.

While you may never want to manipulate others yourself, you may find that the insight of understanding why is critical, especially if you are in the position of healing from a relationship with one such person. When you are able to understand the other person's mind, you may be able to recognize it for what it truly is—disordered.

Beyond just that, though, the insight provided in understanding dark psychology allows us to see what made us so vulnerable to its grasp in the first place. You will be able to see exactly why these problems arise. You will know what it is that each of these techniques plays off of, and in knowing what they use, you can figure out how to shield from them.

Consider that NLP directly influences the unconscious mind. When you know that the unconscious mind is one of the most commonly attacked parts of the mind when trying to influence someone else, you can remind yourself to always do self-checks, understanding why you do what you are doing at any time. You can ask yourself if the behaviors that you are doing at that moment are your own, or if they are common for people that are usually manipulated. You can figure out if the thought in your mind that is driving you is your own, or if it seems out of place, or contradictory to a though that you know that you have had for ages.

Effectively, when you are able to recognize the thought processes of yourself in relation to dark psychology, you can figure out whether you have been manipulated in the past. Knowing that is critical to recognizing if you are actually a victim or if you are proactive enough to avoid victimization altogether.

What is true, despite the insight that you have gained, however, is that, you have earned knowledge. You have knowledge of what is possible in the world. You have knowledge about the mind and some of its secrets. You have knowledge about the predators that you may never have been aware of in reality. That is invaluable. Knowledge is power, and if you can wield that power bravely and proudly, you will be able to protect yourself.

CHAPTER 8: NLP FOR A SUCCESSFUL LIFE

Finally, we have reached the last chapter in this book. You may be feeling like you have far more insight into how you can use NLP and influence other people. However, you can also use it on yourself as well. Do you have some sort of negative trauma that makes it difficult for you to function? Perhaps you feel like you have been held back by your emotions or attempts to get through life. Well, after reading this book, you now have several tools that can help you feel better about who you are, what you want, and how you live life. All you need to do is begin to utilize them.

NLP can be used upon yourself regularly enough to make yourself happier, healthier, and more confident. In attracting happiness and confidence, you will find that you are far more successful in your endeavors. You may realize that you are able to better communicate and relate to people after having defeated your anxiety or fears. You may find that you are able to get along better because you can communicate easier. You may find that you are simply feeling better without that concern over how people will see you is gone.

When you are able to wield NLP for yourself, you can begin to defeat any traumas that have lingered, holding you back for far too long. You will be able to reframe those traumas, separating from that negativity and figuring out ways to make those memories something far less traumatic. You will be able to anchor yourself in a process that is incredibly similar to the one used for other people, and with using this, you will find that you are able to defeat negative habits. With those habits gone, you will feel far more capable. You will be empowered. You will be successful. You will be using NLP for its truest purpose—to wield to help others and yourself.

This chapter will guide you through three techniques that you can use to wield the power of NLP on yourself. You will learn how to use dissociation in order to distance yourself from feelings related to a specific traumatic event or to remove a trigger between an event and a feeling. You will learn to use reframing to change the way that you view an event or memory. Lastly, you will be guided through how to anchor yourself with ease.

Dissociation

Anxiety can be debilitating, especially if it is an anxiety toward something that you must face regularly. Let's go back to the example of the woman who had an accident in front of her class and could never get past it again. She may decide, after reading through this book, that she wants to go through the process of dissociation. She wants to figure out how to remove that inherent link between her negative feelings and being able to go in front of crowds once and for all.

This process involves three simple steps: Identify the problematic emotion, focus on it and the cause, and then visualize and change.

Identify emotion → Focus on that emotion's trigger → Visualize the trigger → Change the trigger's context in your mind

Our friend may identify that she feels shame. She is ashamed that she urinated on herself in class in front of all of her peers, and that shame comes up regularly. She acknowledges that she feels that same shame every time she stands in front of other people, such as her coworkers, or when she has to go to an interview, and in the back of the mind, she is always afraid that it will happen again.

Next, she must visualize the triggering event. In this case, she visualizes the incident like it was yesterday—she stops and remembers how she felt when she had to go to the restroom but was too afraid to raise her hand and ask to go. She had been embarrassed that she was going to go during a presentation, and she worried that those around her would be angry that she did not hear the presentation that was given. She imagines elementary school her going up to the front of the class, trying desperately to give her own presentation, even though she really needed to go to the restroom. She hears the sound of the rain pitter-pattering on the window in the classroom, and she remembers the sensation of wet warmth spreading down her legs. She remembers the sound of laughter that exploded within the room and the embarrassment and tears as she ran to the bathroom, with urine squelching in her shoes. She remembers this as vividly as possible, and she can feel her face turning bright red in shame as she does.

With the memory firmly in mind, it is time to repeat that scene again, but this time, trying to distance herself from the shame that she felt. It is time for her to look at the memory in a way that reduces the negativity. Perhaps she imagines that *everyone* wet their pants at the same time, and the laughter was directed toward everyone, not just her. Maybe she imagines that instead of urine, she had spilled soda or something else on her lap. She wants to change the context, so it is no longer distressing and instead funny.

Over time, the negative emotions will fade away. It may take time and repetition, but over time, the feelings of shame will be desensitized and fade away.

Content Reframing

Another technique that can be useful toward yourself is learning to reframe the content. You will effectively be taking the feeling that you want to eliminate and reframing what has happened in order to change the result. This is effectively attempting to tap into the cycle of thoughts, feelings, and behaviors. For example, if you feel like you are a bad person, you are going to act in ways that fail to show that you are a good person—you will be nervous and flighty. This will lead other people to want to keep their distance, only further reinforcing that initial thought of being a bad person.

When you are able to remove that initial negative feeling, so you stop obsessing, you will see a change in behavioral patterns as well. For example, let's go back to the woman who urinated in class as a child. She is so concerned with embarrassing herself in public again that she gets afraid every time he knows that she has to perform or give a presentation. This leads to nervousness, which leads to a failure to perform to satisfaction, which further reinforces her fear.

In reframing, you will effectively stop focusing on the negative and instead shift your attention to something else that will help, such as accepting your own responsibility for your emotions. You may decide that you will no longer worry about failing or making a mistake and instead focus on how to ensure that your project is as successful as possible. In doing so, you will actually shift your attention to something that you can fix. In the end, you will perform better and teach yourself that the shift in attention is absolutely necessary. You will find that life gets better and that you actually are not as afraid of presentations as you initially were because you have begun to get some positive experiences out of it.

Anchoring Yourself

Finally, the last process that will be discussed within this book is how to anchor yourself. You will be able to use that anchoring process with all of the benefits of anchoring that was discussed earlier and begin to apply it to yourself as well. The only real difference in anchoring yourself versus anchoring others is that when you anchor yourself, much more of the process is internal. You do not have to try to trigger emotions in other people—instead, you are focused on yourself and what you need to do.

This will follow the same steps as anchoring other people: You will still be making it a point to identify an emotion, identifying a trigger for the emotion, identifying an anchor, triggering the emotion, and then using the anchor until it works. That stays the same. What changes are the methods through which you are able to anchor other people? Instead of focusing on how to trigger the feelings in other people externally, you must trigger them within yourself.

For example, consider our friend who had the accident once more. Perhaps she wants to stop feeling anxious and instead feel relaxed when she is presenting. She declares that the feeling that she wishes to trigger is relaxation. She then must think of a time during which she felt that emotion incredibly strongly in order to use it. Perhaps she chooses a time on her wedding night during which she and her newlywed husband watched the sunset over the ocean to the sound of the waves lapping at the beach. That time was particularly relaxing for her and she loved it. That memory becomes her trigger for her emotion.

Now, she chooses a simple anchor—she decides to use a very specific tapping pattern of her toes against the bottom of her shoe, as she knows that it will be discreet, and she will be able to use it in public without anyone ever knowing.

She thinks about that memory at the beach, waiting for the feelings of relaxation to wash over her, and right as those emotions reach their peak, she taps her toes within her shoe to the pattern she is linking to the memory. Over the course of several days and attempts at this, she finds that every time she taps her toes, she is reminded of that relaxing memory. She has now anchored herself to that feeling and can use it any time she is in public and feeling distressed, or whenever she has to present for someone at work. She can use these techniques and find that her stress and anxiety simply melt away.

CONCLUSION

Congratulations! That brings us to the end of **Dark Psychology Secrets**. Hopefully, as you read, you found the content to be compelling, interesting, informative, and easy to follow. With care, this book was designed to guide you through the world of dark psychology.

Dark psychology is the look into the minds of the most heinous, monstrous humans that exist. When you are looking into the depths of dark psychology, you are looking into the minds of those who are out to hurt others. Serial killers, master manipulators, and abusers alike may share these traits, and those traits make them particularly dangerous. What is worse, however, is that these people understand psychology. They understand exactly how they need to interact with other people in order to be seen as charismatic and trustworthy enough to win a spot in the hearts of their victims and targets. The dark psychology user is able to do this simply by knowing how to manipulate their target in just the right way.

CPSIA information can be obtained
at www.ICGtesting.com
Printed in the USA
BVHW040632260321
603504BV00009B/453